Dream Again

A 30 Day Journey to Dream Once Again

A Sisterhood Collaboration

Justeina Brownlee, Stephanie Lammers, Betsy Baringer, Jess
Rosebrook, Michelle Osborne, Erin Killion, Brittani Lime, Heather
Westrick, Leslie Meyer, Janet Conley, Crystal Barnett, Valentine Pitts,
Adelynn Lammers, Marti Garrett, Kelly Hopson

Published by
Brave Sisterhood publications

© 2019 · Brave Sisterhood

Dedication

This devotional is dedicated to each of you that took the time to believe in each of us. Without your encouragement and support, we would have never stepped out into all that God had planned for our lives. You have stirred up the gifts on the inside of us and infused our hearts with courage. We are so honored that you took the time to speak that kind of life into our worlds. We love you... although you aren't called by name in this dedication, you know who you are.

Day 1

See It

But forget all that—it is nothing compared to what I'm going to do! For I'm going to do a brand-new thing. See, I have already begun! Don't you see it? I will make a road through the wilderness of the world for my people to go home and create rivers for them in the desert! ***Isaiah 43:18-19 TLB***

Sometimes dreaming can be hard. Whether you are a risk taker or the "play it safe" type, dreaming is scary. But why? In my opinion, it's because we have a hard time seeing the dream. While we want to see the dream with our eyes, God first shows us the dream in our hearts. While we start trying to figure out HOW it's going to happen, God is first trying to get us to see WHAT can happen. In Isaiah 43:18, God asks, "Don't you see it?" Of course, He's not talking about with our physical eyes, but instead with our spiritual eyes- with our hearts.

The first step to reaching a dream that God places in our hearts is to SEE IT. It says in scripture about Abraham in Genesis 15:4–6: "Then the LORD said to him, 'No, your servant will not be your heir, for you will have a son of your own who will be your heir.' Then the LORD took Abram outside and said to him, 'Look up into the sky and count the stars if you can. That's how many descendants you will have!' And Abram believed the LORD, and the LORD counted him as righteous because of his faith." God had placed the dream of having a son in Abraham and Sarah's hearts. The problem was that they were well past the age of being able to have any children. While they were still trying to figure out HOW it could happen, God wanted them to see WHAT could happen. So, the Bible says, God takes Abraham outside and tells him to look up at the stars and try to count them, because that's how many children he would have. He asked Abraham to SEE IT; to see the dream of having a son in his heart. To believe that God was going to do it, even if he wasn't sure how. If you and I get stuck at how, we will never be able to see what. It happens to us all the time. I believe as we begin to dream again the first step will be to SEE IT.

Don't allow yourself to begin questioning how something can happen when God places an idea or dream in your heart. Whether your dream is to have a baby like Abraham, or maybe to start a business, to step out in ministry, to lose a few dozen pounds, or to fix your broken marriage. Whatever that dream is...you have to first SEE IT. Allow God to show you in your heart what he can do. Don't question, don't doubt, don't fear...just SEE. As you begin to see it, you can follow God's instruction in Habakkuk 2:2-3, 'And then God answered: "Write this. Write what you see. Write it out in big block letters so that it can be read on the run. This vision-message is a witness pointing to what's coming."' As God allows you to see it in your heart, write down what He's showing you.

There's something powerful that happens as we take what we see in our hearts and begin to put it down on paper in the natural. Something supernatural in fact, faith begins to rise in us. It's much like the response Abraham had to God as he began to SEE that God would give him a son. The Bible says that as he looked at the stars, "Abram believed the LORD, and the LORD counted him as righteous because of his faith." Abraham believed God. That's the only response God needs from us. The rest is up to Him. First, you have to SEE IT.

Reflection

1. What's usually stopping you from dreaming bigger?

2. What's one crazy dream that you haven't even considered simply because you couldn't figure out HOW it could happen?

Application

1. In the back of this book there is a DREAM bucket list just for you! Write down one dream that God has placed in your heart that you've never spoken out loud. Begin to write your dreams down as God gives them to you over the next 30 days. Don't figure out HOW, just SEE it and write it down.

Justeina Brownlee

Day 2
Distracted Dreaming

'But Martha was distracted by all the preparations that had to be made. She came to him and asked, "Lord, don't you care that my sister has left me to do the work by myself? Tell her to help me!"' **Luke 10:40**

Have you ever been driving somewhere and all of a sudden, you're at a different spot? You had so many other things on your mind that without even thinking about it, you were suddenly at your destination? I know that we would never want to admit that this has happened to us, but I bet you can relate to that feeling. The fact is, we get distracted. We get distracted with other thoughts, things that need done, busy schedules, kids, friends, husbands, the list could go on and on. We go about our day and follow our routine without even thinking. We're thinking about other things that need to get done and we're distracted from the task we're doing. This made me wonder, am I dreaming distracted? Is God giving me glimpses of dreams, little snippets of the future He has for me, but I am living so distracted by small, insignificant, busy things that I'm missing out on the bigger, better dream God has for me? I've heard it said that if the enemy can't stop you, he will make you too busy. Too busy to follow the call God has placed on your life. Too busy to hear His still small voice. Too busy to dream. Too busy, too distracted.

The Bible gives us the perfect example of focusing on what is important versus being distracted by the busyness of life. In Luke 10:40 it says 'But Martha was distracted by all the preparations that had to be made. She came to him and asked, "Lord, don't you care that my sister has left me to do the work by myself? Tell her to help me!"' It makes me wonder, how many times do we get frustrated that others around us are following what God has called them to do, while we are distracted by our busyness? Martha was distracted from Jesus. By what? By serving her guests. Why? Because she was anxious. Anxious about what? Anxious about feeding everyone, and in all likelihood, anxious about what everyone would think of her and her household if she didn't do it well.

But Martha didn't recognize her distraction until Jesus helped her see her heart. She thought she was doing the right thing by serving everyone. But Jesus pointed out to Martha that her values were out of order. She had shifted her attention from the greater importance to the lesser. So, in our busyness, we must ask, what is the real distraction? What does our heart desire? Are we choosing "the good portion," seeking the great "one thing" (Psalm 27:4), or something less?

It became very obvious to me just the other day how distracted I am going through my everyday life. I would say that most days I am a Martha and miss the God opportunities right in front of me. I was in the kitchen making lunch and all of a sudden I heard my little four-year-old daughter shouting at me "Mom! Mom! Are you even listening?" She had been going on and on about a story she wanted to tell me, and I couldn't even concentrate for just a couple of minutes because I was too distracted. It was almost as if God shook me in that moment and made me realize, I couldn't even take a couple of minutes to listen to my precious daughter who I prayed and asked God for, what was I doing that was more important? Sadly, I was thinking about cleaning that needed to get done around the house and errands that I needed to run. I was distracted.

Proverbs 4:45 says "Keep your eyes straight ahead; ignore all sideshow distractions." Distractions are going to come. Life is going to get busy. Demands for our time and attention are going to feel heavy. But where are our eyes? Are they darting left and right, up and down, watching every single thing trying to keep all of the balls up in the air? Or are they straight ahead on the One who holds the answers, has the plan, and wants to give us the dream?

Reflection

1. What are 3 things that seem like they are important, but are really causing a distraction in your life?

Application

1. Distractions are going to come. How are you going to respond to these things? Come up with a game plan to get them done but not allow them to overtake the important in your life.

2. Think about a time when you were a Martha, rushing, busy and missed out on the important event in front of you. How did you feel? Think about a time when you were a Mary, saw the significance of what was happening in front of you and let go of other distractions. How did you feel? Make up your mind to be sensitive to God's voice and ask Him to reveal the moments to you when you get distracted and He needs your attention.

Betsy Baringer

Day 3
Don't Burn Out

"Don't burn out, keep yourselves fueled and aflame!" ***Romans 12:12 MSG***

"I'm so burnt out! I don't think I can keep doing this." I've heard those exact words from countless women over the years, and I have had the same thought too. Burnout is a real thing and it can happen to the best of us. If you haven't experienced it yet, there will most likely be a day coming when you're trucking through life, attempting to do the best you can, and you find yourself completely wiped out. If this is you today, you're not alone. Know that there's HOPE for your season and things can turn-a-round.

In Romans 12:12 (NIV), scripture tells us, "Be joyful in hope." I can recall reading this many times and often finding myself puzzled over HOW to actually do it. How do I remain joyful in hope? According to Webster's dictionary, hope means a strong belief that something will happen or be the case in the future or a belief that someone will or should achieve something.

One day in my study time, I read the Message translation of that exact same verse and the light bulb went on in my mind! It says, "Don't burn out, keep yourselves fueled and aflame!" Romans 12:12 (MSG)
THAT WAS IT! That was the secret to remaining joyful in hope. I had to learn how to avoid burn out and keep fueled up. But, how?! The problem is, we live in a day and age where the 'norm' is to hustle, hustle, hustle, but this so often leads to running around breathless and worn out...burned out!

Hebrews 12:1-3 says, "Therefore, since we are surrounded by such a huge crowd of witnesses to the life of faith, let us strip off every weight that slows us down, especially the sin that so easily trips us up. And let us run with endurance the race God has set before us. We do this by keeping our eyes on Jesus, the champion who initiates and perfects our faith. Because of the joy awaiting him, he endured the cross, disregarding its shame. Now he is seated in the place of honor beside God's throne. Think of all the hostility he endured from sinful people; then you won't become weary and give up." These verses include two crucial instructions that teach us how to avoid burn out and stay fueled up:

1.   Strip Off Weights Tripping Us Up

Weights don't always show up in huge ways, like blaring sin; sometimes they can be masked in subtle things like discontentment, jealousy, pride and envy. The reality is though, they will weigh us down each and every time. A few months ago, I decided to step out and take a run with my son's weighted belt. At first, it felt pretty manageable. It didn't seem to slow me down until I got to about mile one, then the weight started to feel unbearable. I couldn't believe how a simple ten-pound weighted vest could slow me down and ultimately stop my run. Before I knew it, I was walking and no longer running. My body could NOT keep up with the extra pounds. That day it was an eye opener to me. This is how it is when we attempt to run this race God has us on while carrying the weight of sin on us.

2.   Change Our View

How can we fulfill the dreams God has placed inside of us, if we're stuck watching everyone else live out theirs? It's easy to do. It only takes a few minutes of scrolling through social media and before you know it, we are comparing our real life with someone else's highlight reel. No one is living their best life. Let me repeat that...NO ONE is living their best life without real life struggles and hardships. No one is living out their dreams in a perfect world. It doesn't exist. Yes, some are further along than we are in areas and we can be inspired and empowered by them, but we cannot fix our view on others. It will mess with us every single time. Our view must be set on the One who births the dreams within us and who brings those dreams to a reality. His name is Jesus. And the encouraging thing is, He has His eye on us as well, to strengthen us and give us the wisdom we need as we take steps towards all He has for us.

When we are on this journey of dreaming again, we must remember that the enemy, the devil, is on a mission to get us disheartened. He wants us to faint, run out of steam, get weary, stop running the race, or worse yet, never begin at all. He attempts to trip us up by using weariness to prevent us from reaching our destiny. The devil's goal is to take us out, cripple us and stop us from understanding where our strength comes from! And his tactic is to do anything to weigh us down and get our eyes off of Jesus. Not today Satan. We're onto your schemes. Let's do our part to strip off the weight and change our view.

Reflection

1. What areas in your life do you see the enemy attempting to weigh you down and burn you out?

2. How can you aggressively rid this area/area(s) from your life to keep yourself fueled?

Application

1. Prayerfully take 1-2 steps to keep your eyes focused on Jesus. (ex. Turn off social media and phone during devotional time, find an accountability friend to help encourage and keep you focused.)

Stephanie Lammers

Day 4
Don't Follow Your Dreams

Then he said to all, "Anyone who wants to follow me must put aside his own desires and conveniences and carry his cross with him every day and keep close to me! **Luke 9:23 TLB**

The Follow Test. Has God ever given you one? The truth is that as we embark on a journey together about "dreaming again", about believing the impossible, about reaching for the stars; we have to start our journey with taking a *Follow Test*. The reason we need to take a follow test is because nowhere in scripture does Jesus instruct us to "follow our dreams". He simply commands us to follow Him. And sometimes in the dreaming process we can get off track and take our eyes off Jesus, the author of all dreams. In our pursuit of our dream we can find ourselves overwhelmed, exhausted, confused, and ready to give up. But it's not because the dream is too hard, it's because we've somehow lost sight of Jesus and begun to dream in our own strength. Jesus tells us in Luke 9:23 to "keep close to him".

Recently we went on a vacation with all three of our children. We had to fly to our destination. When we arrived at the airport, I gathered all the kids and gave them the "stay close to me" speech. I explained to them that there were going to be crowds of people in the airport and I needed them to keep close to me. That I should always be able to see them, and they should always be able to see me. We started our trek through the large airport and as we went, I frequently peeked over my shoulder to make sure I had all three of them close to me. As we kept pressing on toward the gate, I noticed the gap between me and my 9-year-old was getting larger and larger. Frustrated, I stopped, and in my mom voice explained to him that if he doesn't close the gap and stay close to me, he could get lost in the crowd. That if he doesn't close the gap, he may take a wrong turn. That if he doesn't close the gap, he may get on the wrong airplane. That if he doesn't close the gap, an enemy may take him from me. That if he doesn't close the gap, we may miss the plane and never make it to the destination we are headed to.

As I thought back on that time in the airport I wondered if Jesus sometimes does the same thing with each of us. I wonder if he looks back over His shoulder and notices that the gap between us and Him is getter larger and larger. And I wonder if he would say to us "I need you to keep close to me. If you don't close the gap, you may get lost in the crowd. If you don't close the gap, you may take a wrong turn. If you don't close the gap, you may get on the wrong plane. If you don't close the gap, the enemy may take you out. If you don't close the gap, you may not make it to the destination I have planned for you." The Follow Test. It's important in this pursuit of dreaming that we are following Jesus and not our dreams. That we are following Jesus and not our desires. That we are following Jesus and not our own pursuits. That we are following Jesus and not a sign. That we are following Jesus and not a good idea. While you dream...And I want you to; don't take your eyes off of Jesus. Keep close to Him. The truth is that if we will keep close to Jesus, He will lead us straight to our dreams and destination.

Reflection

1. Have you ever had a gap between you and Jesus? Give an example.

2. How can you keep close to Jesus while pursuing your Dream?

Application

1. Allow God to give you a "Follow Test". Today spend some time asking God to search your heart and life and close any gap that there may be between you and Jesus. As God stirs your dreams through this devotional, make a commitment to keep close to Jesus.

Justeina Brownlee

Day 5
Give God Your Dream

*In her deep anguish Hannah prayed to the LORD, weeping bitterly. And she made a vow, saying, "LORD Almighty, if you will only look on your servant's misery and remember me, and not forget your servant but give her a son, then I will give him to the LORD for all the days of his life, and no razor will ever be used on his head." **1 Samuel 1:10-11***

Every girl's dream growing up is to have that "Happily ever after" life. The one where you fall in love with Prince Charming, have the fairy tale wedding with all the bells and whistles. He then sweeps you away to his castle, you have beautiful kids, and live happily ever after. The End.

As ladies, we know this is far from the truth or maybe this did happen for you, Praise the Lord. Far too often we don't hear of the hardship in acquiring a dream like this. The hurt, the pain, the brokenness, and the list can go on that you had to endure. We know for sure that Hannah did not have that happily ever after life. She had to share her husband, she was considered as the lesser wife by her rival because she was unable to bear kids. The stigma of being barren in that culture was unbelievable. You were despised, mocked, rejected and you were the hot topic at every women's gathering. I could only imagine how Hannah felt. I don't believe Hannah dreamt about having a life like this. She had dreams just like every other woman.

Often times there will be hardship between you and your dream. There will be a dry desert, where there seems to be no life, no vegetation, no growth. The desert is only there to condition us to live the dream. Hannah had her fair share of hardship. She went through her desert. And so many times through these hardships and deserts we lose sight of the dream. But I want to encourage you, hold on to your dream whatever it is. Don't lose hope, don't listen to the noise around you, don't get discouraged by those that don't support you. Keep believing, keep trusting. God is about to blow your mind. What can we learn from Hannah to help us make our dream a reality:

First, she was a committed woman and constant in prayer. (1Sam 1:10,12) Hannah didn't complain about her hardship, she prayed about it. It is important to know that during your dry season of not seeing anything growing that the Lord of the Harvest is on our side. When no one else understands what you are going through, God understands. He is the one that gave you that dream and He knows what it requires to make it a reality. Consult Him. He hears your heart's cry and blesses you according to your desire in alignment to His will. Hannah's prayer life was the foundation she held onto going through her season of uncertainty. When there is nothing else to do – pray, and after you have done that, pray again! At the very end, she got God's blessing and a great reward.

Second, she was the Lord's humble servant. (1Sam: 16,18) Many times when we are in a place where we don't see anything going on with our dream, it seems as though God is not answering your prayer or He is taking too long. It's easy for us to lean on our own understanding and try creating our own dream. And most of the time it is out of God's will. Hannah made herself vulnerable to the Lord. In the midst of believing in your dream, pride could step in and distract you from fulfilling what God has planned for you. Depression could overwhelm you and make your situation seem impossible and stop you from believing. But instead, place everything aside, humble yourself and trust the process. He who began a good work in you is able to complete it (Philippians 1:6). Don't become bitter and let pride rear his ugly head, rather become better in humbling yourself before the Lord and trusting His process. He will never fail you and He is not a man that He should lie (Numbers 23:19).

Reflection

1. What is God asking you to sacrifice in order for Him to bless your dream?

Application

1. Ask God to reveal what is holding you back from believing in your dream again?

2. Look and ask God to show you three verses in the bible. Use these verses to speak into your dream. God wants to make your dream become a reality. Are your ready to dream?

Valentine Pitts

Day 6
Share It

*Then I told them about the desire God had put into my heart, and of my conversation with the king, and the plan to which he had agreed. They replied at once, "Good! Let's rebuild the wall!" And so the work began. **Nehemiah 2:18***

Why is it that so many dreams go unfulfilled? Why do so many dreams never take flight? Maybe it's because the dreamer kept the dream all to themselves. Don't underestimate the power of a shared dream. There's something that happens when we share the dream on our heart with a trusted friend. It can bring accountability, courage, resources, wisdom, and faith for what's on the inside of us.

For Nehemiah, God had placed the dream of rebuilding a broken city on his heart. The Bible says that as Nehemiah heard about his old city that was in ruins, he began to get a burden to rebuild it back up. The funny thing about a dream is that it isn't always an exciting, whimsical idea. Sometimes it's an overwhelming and heavy burden for something that needs to be made right. That was the case for Nehemiah. After Nehemiah began to be burdened for the dream of rebuilding the city, the first thing he did, after much prayer, was SHARE IT.

Nehemiah, at the time, was a cupbearer to the king, which is just a fancy way of saying he made sure nothing was poisoned before the king drank it. The first person Nehemiah decided to share the dream with was his boss, the King. Nehemiah 2:5 says, *Then I prayed to the God of heaven, and I answered the king, "If it pleases the king and if your servant has found favor in his sight, let him send me to the city in Judah where my ancestors are buried so that I can rebuild it."* Why did Nehemiah pray to God right before sharing it? Because he knew he could lose his life if the King didn't like what he was sharing. It took courage for Nehemiah to share the dream. It will take courage for you to share your dream too. It may feel silly, it may feel uncomfortable, it may even feel terrifying, but to cause your dream to take flight, you're going to have to share it.

Not only did Nehemiah share the dream with his boss, but he also shared it with friends that would help him fulfill the dream.

Always remember you may be just one resource away from fulfilling your dream and that resource will come through those you share it with. In fact, it says in Nehemiah 2:16-17, *The officials did not know where I had gone or what I was doing, because as yet I had said nothing to the Jews or the priests or nobles or officials or any others who would be doing the work. Then I said to them, "You see the trouble we are in: Jerusalem lies in ruins, and its gates have been burned with fire. Come, let us rebuild the wall of Jerusalem, and we will no longer be in disgrace."* The truth was that the very people that would help Nehemiah do the work of the dream were the ones he had to share the dream with.

As Nehemiah began to be burdened with a dream, he prayerfully began to share it with others. He allowed God to lead him to share it with the right people at the right time. He shared it with the king and the king responded with releasing him to go, as well as giving him all the resources he needed to rebuild the city. He shared it with his friends and they responded with, 'we are with you, let's rebuild the city together'. My favorite words of the entire story come in verse 18 of Nehemiah 2. It says, "So they began this good work." That, my friend, is the power of sharing your dream. The good work can finally begin.

Reflection

1. What scares you the most about sharing your dream?

2. Who are two people you need to share your dream with?

Application

1. Today set a time with a friend and share a few of the dreams that you have on your heart. Whether it's a big idea, a broken place of your life that needs mended, or a burden God has given you. The best next step to seeing the work begin is to share it.

Justeina Brownlee

Day 7
But I Can't....

But Moses pleaded with the Lord, "O Lord, I am not very good with words. I never have been, and I'm not now, even though you have spoken to me. I get tongue-tied, and my words get tangled."
Exodus 4:10 NLT

I remember so clearly the day I came across this verse in the Bible. I had just had my second brain surgery. A surgery that took my speech… but it took far more than just my speech. It took my confidence to speak, which in turn, took my dream. After extensive speech therapy, I regained my speech. But, I had lost my confidence, which crushed my dream. My dream was to share my story with the world….and to share it by telling others of the miracle God had done in my life. I wanted to give others hope and help them understand their role in receiving their miracle. But now...even though I had regained my speech, I stuttered, I got confused, and I repeated myself. Not exactly a candidate to be sharing my story and giving anyone hope. Did I really want to get up in front of anyone like that? NO WAY! I didn't want to embarrass myself or God. I was heartbroken. Wasn't this what God had called me to do? Wasn't this my mission? Wasn't this why God had given me so many more years than what the doctors told me I had? I was certain that this was my calling, that this was my mission, but my insecurities and all of my fears of failure were going to keep me from my dream.

The scripture continues on in Exodus 4:11-12, "Then the Lord asked Moses, "Who makes a person's mouth? Who decides whether people speak or do not speak, hear or do not hear, see or do not see? Is it not I, the Lord? Now go! I will be with you as you speak, and I will instruct you in what to say." Ok, you have my attention now God. I'm listening.

So, you're telling me that if I put myself out there God, you'll guide my words, you'll guide my mouth? Then sign me up! My dream was alive again! I had replaced the lie I was believing, the lie no one even told me! My thoughts were 'I can't, I stutter, I repeat myself, my words get twisted and tangled', and I replaced it with God's words, his truth: "Jessie, you CAN do this. Jessie, I will guide your words, I will speak for you, just take the next step, walk in faith, not in fear."

How often do we let our own insecurities get in the way of our dreams? Our own....yes OUR insecurities. God never wanted us to be crippled by fear. He wants us to be dreaming of the impossible, dreaming of what we don't think is possible because then we have to rely on Him! He is the only way our dreams are possible! We can't make our dreams happen, only He can!

I had a few speaking opportunities along the way before my second surgery that took my speech...but then after that surgery I allowed myself to be crippled by fear of doing that ever again. Until one day, about 5 years after that surgery I was given the opportunity to share again. The first time since I had lost my speech, the first time since I had been working so hard to put my trust in God and overcome my fears. I had to wait 5 years! I am the most impatient person so 5 years was about 5 years too long for me! Anyone who is that patient is just weird.

What happened in those 5 years? I endured. For many years, I have chosen 1 word to focus on for that year. Well, for several of those 5 years my word was endure. Yes, I used it over and over because I needed it for most of those years as I waited for the opportunity to share my story.

Here is what I did for those 5 years:
1. I overcame the lie with God's truths
2. I stayed focused on my dream
3. I persevered through the struggles and the roadblocks
4. I dug into scripture like never before
5. I prayed for it

God dreams will prosper!

Reflection

1. What is it that you are dreaming of?

2. What's stopping you from it?

Application

1. TODAY, whatever is stopping you, find a scripture or 2 or 3 that you will use to defeat that lie every time you start to doubt that you can do it or begin to believe it's not possible!

Jess Rosebrook

Day 8
Expectantly Waiting

Wait and hope for and expect the Lord; be brave and of good courage and let your heart be stout and enduring. Yes, wait for and hope for and expect the Lord. **Psalm 27:14 AMPC**

Have you ever felt like God placed an exciting, big dream on your heart, but then it didn't come to fruition right away? That there was this dream you couldn't wait to see come true, and yet you kept waiting? I think we've all experienced that at some point in our lives. It can be discouraging when we know God has given us a dream, but then we don't get to see it come to pass right away. It's time to have a mental shift in the way we view these times!

One of the amazing things about our God is that He never requires us to go through a situation without also providing us encouragement and support through scripture. Waiting on our dream is no different. Isaiah 25:1 says "Lord, you are my God; I will exalt you and praise your name, for in perfect faithfulness you have done wonderful things, things planned long ago." Joshua 21:45 says "Not one of all the Lord's good promises to Israel failed; every one was fulfilled." And Hebrews 6:15 says "And so after waiting patiently, Abraham received what was promised." I realize none of these scriptures mention a dream, but if God has placed a dream in our heart then He's also given us a promise that He will fulfill it. If the dream is a God-given dream, and not just one we've decided on our own, then God will make it come to pass. It might not happen when we think it should happen, and it might not all play out the way we envisioned it, but our God is faithful. Our God keeps His promises. Our God will bring the dream to life.

So, as we're waiting for the dream to come to life, what do we do? We should "Wait *and* hope for *and* expect the Lord; be brave *and* of good courage and let your heart be stout *and* enduring. Yes, wait for *and* hope for *and* expect the Lord." (Psalm 27:14 AMPC). We are to wait expectantly! We wait believing that the dream could come to life at any time. But we also need to make sure that while we're expectantly waiting, we don't become stagnant. God might be giving you a dream for something in your future, and there's a time of waiting before the dream comes to life because He needs you to take some action for the dream. That's part of waiting expectantly. When you're expecting a guest to come to your house, you prepare your house for the guest. Our lives shouldn't be any different. When we're expectantly waiting for our dream to come to life, we should be preparing for our dream! Maybe you're single and your dream is to be a wife... so while you're expectantly waiting, begin to take steps to learn how to be a godly wife. Read what God says about being a wife, align your heart with that, and trust that in His timing God will fulfill the promise. Maybe your dream is to be the CEO of a company... so in your expectant waiting, prepare for that position. Develop the character qualities necessary for that position. Begin to network and develop the people skills required to be a CEO.

Whatever your dream is and however long you might wait to see the dream come to pass, continue to always draw near to God, take action to prepare yourself for the dream, and hope and expect God to fulfill the promise He's given you.

Reflection

1. What dream has God placed in your heart that you've been expectantly waiting to come to pass?

2. Is there anything you could be doing in the waiting to be who God is calling you to be for the dream?

Application

1. Make a list of 1-2 things you could begin to do to prepare yourself for the dream God has placed in your heart. Put the list into action.

Erin Killion

Day 9
The Pruning Process

Every branch in me that does not bear fruit he takes away, and every branch that does bear fruit he prunes, that it may bear more fruit.
John 15:2 (ESV)

Perhaps to a gardener this verse makes sense. To prune, as Webster defines it: 1a: to reduce especially by eliminating superfluous matter 2: to cut off or cut back parts of for better shape or more fruitful growth. So, the gardener or someone with much more of a green thumb than me, knows he must eliminate the "superfluous matter", that which is not necessary or actually *preventing* new growth. To cut back this part does not actually hurt the plant or flower, but will eventually increase its beauty and ability to flourish!

Then why does it seem to hurt humans so much? Pruning or cutting off what is not healthy, life-giving or necessary allows room for more fruitful, beneficial growth. It doesn't always FEEL that way. That's the funny thing about Kingdom work, it doesn't always FEEL good immediately. As we are building and refining this temporal body and mind, it feels like work! It feels like pain! It feels like a gigantic, human-sized bandage being ripped off a nasty open sore! While that might be a bit too much imagery to handle, consider the benefits. God accepts us just as we are, messy make-up running, flaws, yucky pasts, distorted thoughts, sometimes really bad habits. And He already loves us! The neat thing is, He does not choose to leave us stuck in those ruts with wrong thinking and painful, negative cycles. He chooses to encourage us through His Holy Spirit to want MORE, to change!

In this lies the gift of pruning. Certainly, for me it doesn't always FEEL good, it stings actually. Maybe you can relate. Is there an area of your life that is causing you tension in your relationships, something that you continually think you are being criticized for or even a nagging habit you can't quite kick? Asking the Holy Spirit to expose what is not pleasing or offensive can be a difficult question to hear the answer to. Thankfully, He does not leave us alone in this process, but walks with us, loves and encourages us along the way. Deuteronomy 31:6 says: "So be strong and courageous! Do not be afraid and do not panic before them. For the LORD your God will personally go ahead of you. He will neither fail you nor abandon you."

As the dead branches are cut away, the old thoughts, habits and patterns tend to fall along the path. As these raw, exposed spaces are mended and healed, room is made for new growth. The fruits of the spirit now have a place to take root and bud and flourish in what once was a dormant place, too cold or dry and without sustenance to sprout. "But the fruit of the Spirit is love, joy, peace, forbearance, kindness, goodness, faithfulness, gentleness and self-control" Galatians 5:22-23. While these traits are not easily achievable on our own, through the Holy Spirit, progress, not perfection, is attainable. Let's allow the Master Gardener to do what only He can do! Allow the cutting, pruning, and regrowth to begin! Our hope is this: "And I am sure of this, that he who began a good work in you will bring it to completion at the day of Jesus Christ." Philippians 1:6

Reflection

1. Are you comfortable asking God to expose areas in your life that may need to be pruned, or cut out?

2. Do you trust God's good and perfect plan for you? His plan includes making way for more of the gifts He has for you!

Application

1. Ask God to allow a friend to help hold the mirror of truth up for you. Be prepared to endure the pain of truth spoken in love, which will result in a fruitful harvest in due season.

2. Pray for the Holy Spirit to allow your heart to be softened and any blind spots be removed so you may see truth and receive healing.

Michelle Osborne

Day 10
Speak It

...so is my word that goes out from my mouth: It will not return to me empty but will accomplish what I desire and achieve the purpose for which I sent it. **Isaiah 55:11 NIV**

What are you saying about your dream? That thing that God has placed on your heart. That thing that you are burdened to see happen. That thing that you are asking God to do. Yes, that thing. What are you saying about it? Did you know that it matters what you say about it? Our words hold power in them. The Bible says we have the power of life and death in our tongues. It says that the words that come from our mouth are like seeds and they will produce a harvest. Whether it's the harvest we want or not, it is dependent upon the words we are saying. Some of us keep killing our dream before it even starts simply by what we are saying about it. If the only words we are speaking over our dream are words like: 'it's too hard, it will never happen, I'm just not able, they will never'...then that's the harvest we will get.

It's important to God what we speak about our dream. There's a great example in Ezekiel 37. God is asking Ezekiel if he thinks the dead bones in front of him can live again. He in essence was asking Ezekiel, "Do you think this dream can live?" Ezekiel says, I'm not sure only you know God. And then God gives him an important instruction, the scripture says in Ezekiel 37:4-7, '*Then he told me to speak to the bones and say: "O dry bones, listen to the words of God, for the Lord God says, 'See! I am going to make you live and breathe again! I will replace the flesh and muscles on you and cover you with skin. I will put breath into you, and you shall live and know I am the Lord.' So I spoke these words from God, just as he told me to; and suddenly there was a rattling noise from all across the valley, and the bones of each body came together and attached to each other as they used to be.'*
Speak to your dream.

God knows how important it is that we speak to our dream. Not just speak about it, but sometimes you have to speak right to it. If your marriage is a mess and you have a dream to see it healthy, you have to speak to it. Declare God's promises over it. Don't say it will never work, don't say he never will, don't say I just can't...but speak to it. Say to your marriage that it's going to make it, say it's going to be healthy, say that it can be better than ever before, say that your entire family will serve God. You have to speak it. Maybe you have a dream for a new career adventure. Speak it. Don't say I'm not sure how it will work, don't say I'm not smart enough, don't say I don't have what it takes...but speak to it. Say to your dream: if God wants this, He will make it happen, I can do it, nothing is impossible with God, I'm fearfully and wonderfully made for this. You have to speak it.

To say nothing towards the dream is to reap nothing towards the dream. To say words of death towards the dream is to reap death towards the dream. To say life-giving words towards the dream is to reap life towards the dream. It really does matter what you say. Don't say what you see...sometimes what you see with your eyes can be deceptive, but instead remember you will SEE what you SAY. Speak it. And just like Ezekiel, there will suddenly be a rattling noise and you will watch everything come together.

Reflection

1. What have you currently been saying about your dream that may be killing it?

2. What are the new statements you can begin to speak to your dream that will bring it life?

Application

1. Write down two life-giving statements about your dream and commit to declaring those statements every day.

Justeina Brownlee

Day 11
Brace Yourself – Part 1

*"And now, dear brothers and sisters, one final thing. **Fix** your thoughts on what is true, and honorable, and right, and pure, and lovely, and admirable. Think about things that are excellent and worthy of praise."*
Philippians 4:8

I couldn't believe I had agreed to go white water rafting with my husband and four children. Now, don't get me wrong, it had always been a dream of mine and it sure sounded adventuresome and exhilarating. But the closer we got to our destination I started to have second thoughts about the whole idea! My mind began to be flooded with all of the wild unknowns that could happen to us! What if we hit a rock and one of my kids flies out and is greatly injured? What if our guide gets injured out in the middle of this adventure? How in the world will we ever make it back? Talk about crazy thoughts running wild!

We arrived and quickly got our whopping two-minute instruction on how to avoid near death experiences. We bundled up with all of our life saving gear which included a helmet, life preserver and water shoes. All of a sudden, the closer I was getting to this dream of a fabulous time with my family, I wanted to gather my family and sprint back to the car as fast as we could.

Being a mother to four teenagers, I was determined to not show any hint of fear, so I braved up and got in the raft. The trip started so calm and the smooth waters began to take us down this beautiful river when all of a sudden, the leader said something that sort of struck a nerve in me, "Brace yourself! If you don't brace yourself, this could be bad!" Wait? What? Brace yourself, what in the world did he mean?!

He kept saying something that stood out to me the entire experience, "Brace yourself and lean in!" I couldn't believe that when we did those two simple things and obeyed his command, not only did we all stay safely in the raft, but we had an incredible time! Even through the most challenging rapids, we still managed to come through every single time laughing while taking in the nerve-racking experience. It was one of the coolest experiences I've ever encountered! I can't help but think how quickly that dream would have been crushed had I let fear and hesitation take over.

How many of us have had God dreams stir within us and we've shrunk back and didn't get to experience all that He had planned for us?! What I discovered through the white-water rafting experience is that if we truly want to live out the God shaped dreams within us, we must remember to *brace ourselves*.

When you brace yourself, you're not focused on the waves and circumstances coming at you. Instead, you *focus on how tight you are bracing yourself*. If we *focus* on what's ahead: the storms, the relationship issues, the mouthy teenager who is talking back for the millionth time, the fall out argument between you and your husband, the excess pounds you just can't shake, the unknowns of the future; if we focus on those things, we invite fear. And fear will stop and kill our dreams, EVERY SINGLE TIME! In our own strength, we can't change those things, but God can! When we brace ourselves (steady and fix ourselves) in God's truths, faith rises up and pushes fear right out! And He does what only He can do.

Bracing ourselves is *fixing* our minds. If we want to remain fixed and focused, we must start with our minds. We must fix our minds on things on above. Just like I braced my feet in the boat to prevent me from being tossed out, I must daily choose to brace my mindset on the things above, things that are noble, true, full of hope and full of God's truth.

If I'm not **fixing** (bracing) my mind on God thoughts, I will be tossed around in life on a daily basis. Just like being tossed inside the boat could lead to injury, allowing our minds to be tossed around carelessly will also lead to injury.

Reflection

1. What are the areas in your thought life where God wants you to brace yourself in His truths?

2. How can you daily speak life over yourself to help keep your mind fixed on healthy things?

Application

1. Get yourself around someone who can be accountable to you to keep yourself braced and leaned into Him.

2. Find 1-2 Bible verses that you can declare over your mind to keep yourself braced.

Stephanie Lammers

Day 12
Brace Yourself – Part 2

*"And now, dear brothers and sisters, one final thing. **Fix** your thoughts on what is true, and honorable, and right, and pure, and lovely, and admirable. Think about things that are excellent and worthy of praise."*
Philippians 4:8

One of the greatest life lessons I learned that day on that adventurous white-water rafting adventures was how vital it is to not only brace yourself but to truly *lean in*. What I mean by this is, it's not enough to brace yourself without taking the next step, which is leaning into the One who truly brings stability in all areas of life.

There was a man in the Bible by the name of Jeremiah who truly had to learn how to *brace himself* and *lean in*. Jeremiah was called to an assignment. A *tough* assignment. He was called to something extremely bigger than he was and greater than what he felt qualified for. He struggled intensely with feeling inadequate.

Isn't that often what God does with us? He calls us to dreams and assignments that are beyond our human ability! We look at ourselves and think, "Me? I could never do that! I'm not smart enough, patient enough, organized enough," you fill in the blank. In that place when God dropped that assignment and dream in Jeremiah's heart, He spoke these words to Jeremiah,

[17] Brace yourself, Jeremiah!
Stand up, and say to them whatever I tell you to say.
Don't be terrified in their presence,
or I will make you [even more] terrified in their presence.
Today I have made you like a fortified city,
an iron pillar, and a bronze wall.
You will be able to stand up to the whole land.
You will be able to stand up to Judah's kings,
its officials, its priests, and [all] the common people.

They will fight you, but they will not defeat you.
I am with you, and I will rescue you," declares the Lord.
Jeremiah 1:17-19 (GW)

God knew that Jeremiah would be terrified at times when the enemy came at him. The enemy would try and intimidate him and here's the reality; we can all relate to Jeremiah when we feel the enemy's opposition amidst us pursuing our dream. But just like God promised to equip Jeremiah for the assignment, He will equip us as well! When we tenaciously hold fast to the strength of the Holy Spirit, bracing ourselves and leaning into Him, we can take it to the enemy and be an overcomer, every single time! We are stronger than he is. The enemy has nothing on us! The Bible says, "Greater is He that is in us than he who is the world!" (1 John 4:4) God told Jeremiah that He'd make him like a fortified city, a strong pillar of iron!

How do we become so strengthened that we are like a fortified city, a bronze pillar? Truly leaning into Him. *Lean in*. Like *really* lean in. Lean in to God's word. Lean into His love, His presence, His forgiveness, His grace. For years, I went through the motions of reading a devotional or even scripture and my heart was wanting more, but I wasn't really *leaning* in. I wasn't leaning in and coming expectant for what He wanted to teach me, show me, reveal in me. When I wasn't leaning in to His truth, I was receiving little. Little revelation, little breakthrough, little freedoms. It was when I realized that the more I intentionally leaned into His presence in a state of total *humility* and *hunger*, He could then pour into me all that He had in store.

In Psalms 34:4, scripture tells us "God met me more than halfway, he freed me from my anxious fears." I was reading that, and it sort of stopped me in my tracks. "Wait, why would God only meet me halfway? Why wouldn't He come all the way for me to be free?" It was like a revelation dropped from Heaven in that moment. He expects us to take active steps of obedience to meet Him halfway!! We can't just sit around wishing away our problems, fears, anxiety, worry, insecurities, and the many other things that hold us back from moving forward to living out the dreams He's placed within us. We MUST take active steps forward. How? By diving into God's word and asking how we can apply His truths to our lives. Let's decide today that we will tenaciously move forward in the God-sized assignments while *bracing ourselves* and truly *leaning in*!

Reflection

1. What is a dream or 'assignment' that God is stirring in your heart that feels way beyond yourself? (maybe it's working on a broken marriage that looks hopeless, sharing your testimony to bring others to Christ, leading a small group of women in a Bible study, writing a book, etc)

2. How can you practically lean into Him more than ever before?

Application

1. Find 1-2 Bible verses that are applicable to the area you are needing to lean in.

Stephanie Lammers

Day 13
You Go First

Remember this: Whoever sows sparingly will also reap sparingly, and whoever sows generously will also reap generously. ***2 Corinthians 9:6***

I'll never forget the day that I wrote my first book. Okay, well obviously I didn't write the book in one day, but there was THE ONE DAY that I finally started the book. To be honest, writing the book was the easy part; the hard part was starting it. For years, I had the dream of writing a book held up on the inside of me. I had bathed it in prayer and so I also knew it wasn't just my own dream, but in fact was a God dream. So once God had confirmed the dream, naturally I waited for the day a publisher would call me and say "Justeina, God told us you had a book in you and we want to be your publisher and help you get it out." Unfortunately, the days, weeks, and months went by with no call from a publisher.

Now looking back on it, that was such a silly approach. But I think this is the approach we all take with our big dreams. We think that if God gave us this dream, He will certainly tell everyone else and they will make our dream come true. That's only partially true. Actually, while I was waiting on God for my dream…He was waiting on me. He needed me to take the first step. God was saying, "You go first." This is exactly what God told Joshua in the Bible. Joshua had the dream of leading the Israelites to the Promised Land after 40 years of wandering in the desert. And the first obstacle they would have to tackle on their way to the Promised Land would be a flooded Jordan River. Joshua could have just stayed put and waited for God to open the Heavens, waited for God to bring the Promised Land to him. But that's not what God's instruction was. God told him, "You go First."

This was a completely different approach than the Israelites had taken when crossing the Red Sea. First, God parted the waters and then they crossed the sea. This time God told them, you go first. You take the first step. God tells Joshua, *"Now take twelve men from the tribes of Israel, one man from each tribe. When the soles of the feet of the priests carrying the Chest of God, Master of all the earth, touch the*

Jordan's water, the flow of water will be stopped—the water coming from upstream will pile up in a heap." This time they had to take the first step into the flooded water before God would supernaturally part it.

The same was true for me. I had to take the first step towards writing the book before God would supernaturally show up and bring me a publisher. I couldn't wait for the water to part, I had to by faith put my foot into the flooded water and trust God to do the rest. So I did. I began to write a book for which I had no publisher. Maybe no one would ever publish it. Maybe no one would ever read it. But I had to take a step to find out. So one day I sat down, opened up my computer, gave my book a title and began to type out words. Before I knew it I had a page, then a chapter, then many chapters, then finally a publisher. I believe that had I not sat down that ONE DAY and began to take the first step towards the dream, it would still just be a book in my heart.

What about you? What dream is inside of you? What has God confirmed to you? What are you waiting on? Remember, you go first.

Reflection

1. Have you been waiting on God to supernaturally move?

2. Do you think God may be waiting on you?

Application

1. What is one step you could take today towards your dream? Ask God and begin to take that step.

Justeina Brownlee

Day 14
Renewed Hope

"For I know the plans I have for you," says the Lord. "They are plans for good and not for disaster, to give you a future and a hope."
Jeremiah 29:11

Have you ever thought of giving up hope on a situation? Losing hope in your dreams because you have been praying and dreaming them for so long and none of them are coming true? Or you keep praying that a family member would be saved, but they seem to keep walking further away from God?

This happens to me more often than not. Living the busy mom life with four kids, sports activities, homeschooling, planning meals that everyone will like (insert head smack emoji), cleaning house, and not to mention the never-ending amount of laundry- I lose hope. I stop dreaming. I focus so much on the day to day tasks, I lose sight of the things God wants me to accomplish and start feeling defeated. I start giving up hope that I could even complete what He wants me to do. He has called me to do something I cannot do. I'm not strong enough or wise enough. I think He may have the wrong girl!

Now what about giving up hope on your unanswered dreams? Do you think God is ignoring you? Or too busy for you? Absolutely not! God hears you and He's answering. But do we have our hearts open enough to hear Him? Is He trying to pour hope back into your life, but you are ignoring His answers because it's not what you want to hear?

As I'm having all these feelings, the Bible shows me something different. In Jeremiah 29, we are reminded how powerful our God really is. How much He can make happen with the flick of his wrist. God has your back! Are you feeling weak? He will give you power. Are you feeling powerless in your situation? He will give you strength! We just need to have hope and trust in our God.

In this chapter in the book of Jeremiah, Jeremiah wrote a letter to the people who had been taken into exile in Babylon by King Nebuchadnezzar. Within the letter, he told them to build homes, plant gardens, marry and have children. Then to find spouses for their children. He also instructs them to 'seek the peace and prosperity of the city to which I have carried you into exile. Pray to the Lord for it, because if it prospers, you too will prosper.' (Jeremiah 29:7)

Imagine the people being taken captive and the word from God, that you are hoping is a way out, is to pray for the very people and city that took you captive. But, God has a plan and will bring hope! God goes on to say '"When seventy years are completed for Babylon, I will come to you and fulfill my good promise to bring you back to this place.[11] For I know the plans I have for you," declares the Lord, "plans to prosper you and not to harm you, plans to give you hope and a future.' (Jeremiah 29:10-11) This was the message of hope they were waiting for! See, God answers our prayers and renews our hope, but before he renews our hope, we must first have faith in Him and stay committed in what he calls us to do!

Reflection

1.   What is something you have lost hope in? What is a step you can take to walk toward this dream?

2.   God wants us to keep our faith in Him even through struggles or disappointments. Do you have a struggle you have let get the better of you? How has this affected your day to day life? How can you ask God to renew your hope in this struggle?

Application

1.   God is going to test us and give us struggles that may seem hopeless. You first must have faith in your Heavenly Father. Then you must wholeheartedly pray over and over to Him. Just bow your head, lift your arms and open your heart. He will come in and renew your hope.

2. Sometimes it's in our weakest moments when we get the closest to God. That could be exactly what God is wanting too. He is pleading for a close relationship with us. But are we giving that to Him? The harder we pray and ask God to guide us through this process of struggle and defeat, the closer we will get to Him. He is there and He is listening.

Brittani Lime

Day 15
The In Between

"I've picked you, I haven't dropped you. Don't panic, I am with you. There is no need to fear for I'm your God. I'll give you strength. I'll help you. I'll hold you steady, keeping a firm grip on you." **Isaiah 41:9-10**

In between. A time we find ourselves in at some point in our life. It's a time of guessing, insecurity, lack, scarcity, questions and quiet. A time when we ask ourselves, "How did I end up here?". If we look at the before, the beginning of the 'In between', it always starts with a vision, a grand plan about becoming, changing, or transforming ourselves or our circumstances in some way. Perhaps that plan for you is graduating college, getting married, starting a business, being a mom, etc. At the end of the vision, there is always a promise.

Have you ever thought about that specific time between vision and promise- the in between? Why is it so easy to be excited about the dream, but not expect to have to work for it? Here, in this stage of in between, it is easy to question God, to question His calling, to look over our shoulders and wonder would it be better to just go back to where we were or begin to look for our own way out. If I'm being honest, I would say that I despise the in between. However, God has used this exact in between to show my need for it! Sometimes the process of in between feels like failure. Perhaps we feel we have missed God's direction or misheard His voice. At times, in between might feel like a punishment, something we've done wrong and we will proverbially sit in "in between" time out until we've learned our lesson.

Don't get discouraged, God uses the in between to reveal His plan and His dream! Let's face it, our plans are limited to what we know, see, and what we believe can happen in a physical realm. We don't see the plan in its entirety. God uses the in between to make His vision our new dream. His vision opens our world to bigger things that we would have deemed impossible. Have you ever felt like He spoke to you and said, "You will _____", and you thought to yourself "I must have made that up, because that will never happen!". Well, perhaps, that was His vision for you and He will use the in between to show you how He will make it your reality.

Once He has planted the seed of vision, He will emotionally and physically equip us for the task. He has to give us the correct tools and we need time to practice how to use them so we do not go back to what we used to do in crisis mode. He uses the in between to help us find out what we are made of and He challenges us to step up and into a new realm of strength. God uses the in between to change our mindset, to guide us in His way, to prepare us for spiritual battles, to learn to walk in faith, and to recognize that our ability alone won't get the desired outcome.

God gives us the opportunity of in between to recognize his strength. Because in the end, when God works through us, when He gives us a dream, and He equips us with all the tools we need, we recognize that our promise wasn't our plan. We recognize the need for a God who shares His power, His promise and His purpose with us. And when we recognize that we would have, never in a million years, come up with the plan, then we can acknowledge it had nothing to do with us, and everything to do with Him. Hold on ladies, your in between is full of growth, provision, equipment, battles, and fulfilled steps into a divine promise!

Reflection

1. Have you pushed aside a dream because you don't think you can do it?

Application

1. Take time to think about how God has used times of in between in the past to expand your vision of the future.

Heather Westrick

Day 16
Against All Hope, We Hope

Against all hope, Abraham in hope believed and so became the father of many nations, just as it had been said to him, "So shall your offspring be." Without weakening in his faith, he faced the fact that his body was as good as dead—since he was about a hundred years old— and that Sarah's womb was also dead. Yet he did not waver through unbelief regarding the promise of God, but was strengthened in his faith and gave glory to God, being fully persuaded that God had power to do what he had promised. **Romans 4:18-21**

As I read the Bible, it is easy for me to think that the people I read about didn't have to persevere through the 'tough' situations I have to face today. I can find myself saying "But they didn't have to deal with this, and they didn't have to deal with that…I bet no one ever did this to them or posted that about them on social media." But when I really dig down deep, get to know their story, and put myself in their place, I begin to feel their pain, see their struggle, and relate to their story.

One story in particular that has challenged me recently is the story of Abraham and Sarah. Abraham had a promise from God. Have you ever been given a promise? Something that you dreamed about and held close? Something that motivated you when you woke up in the morning and kept you awake at night dreaming about the possibility of it becoming a reality? That's the kind of promise that God gave Abraham. The promise of a son, the promise of decedents, the promise of a future! It didn't happen overnight. It didn't even happen within the next year. Abraham waited years and years…. Almost 30 years to be exact! Now, I don't know about you, but I don't know that I can confidently say I could hold on that long to something that I couldn't see any progress on and actually, something that looked like it was slipping farther and farther away from becoming a reality. But in Romans 4:18-21, Abraham responds this way: *"Yet he did not waver through unbelief regarding the promise of God, but was strengthened in his faith and gave glory to God, being fully persuaded that God had power to do what he had promised"*.

I think we can learn to hold onto two parts of this verse looking at our own dream, our own promise. First of all, the verse begins, "Against all hope, Abraham hoped". When everything was falling apart, he hoped. When everyone told him to give up, he hoped. When every circumstance seemed against him, he hoped. He hoped, and hoped, and held on to his hope. Then when he thought he couldn't go on another day, he found some more hope.

Second, Abraham, "without weakening in his faith, he faced the facts". He took a realistic look at the circumstances in front of him. He knew that he and Sarah were old... not a few gray hairs old, but really old! What circumstances in front of you could get in the way of a promise? Be realistic. Sometimes we need a reality check about where we are, what we are facing, and we need to take some practical steps. But we don't stop there and neither did Abraham and Sarah. The verse goes on to say, "Yet, he did not waver through unbelief, but was strengthened in his faith". So whatever the situation looks like, whatever the report you heard sounds like, whatever your kids are doing now, whatever you think about the marriage that seems like it is failing.... do not waver in your belief! God has given you a promise! Give God the glory for the promise and praise him until you see it come to pass.... because it will - God has the power to do what He has promised!

Reflection

1. What promise has God given you that you are still waiting on?

2. Think back over your life with God. What are some promises that you have seen God come through on? If He came through before, He will come through again!

Application

1. Spend some quiet time with God. Allow yourself to dream. There have been many promises that God has spoken to me over the years that I push away because they don't seem realistic. In the two seconds that I spent thinking about it, I couldn't figure out how to make it happen, so I dismissed it. In this quiet time, dream with God. Let Him speak those promises to you! The best part is, you don't have to do anything but believe God has the power to do what He has promised!

Betsy Baringer

Day 17
Time to Soar

"But those who wait upon God get fresh strength. They spread their wings and soar like eagles. They run and don't get tired, they walk and don't lag behind." ***Isaiah 40:31 MSG***

As an eagle glides through the air, gazing over the land beneath it, this unique bird admires the hard work it took to push through to soar at those utmost heights. Eagles fly higher than any other bird; not because they're better than the other birds, but because they have simply learned to accept who God designed them to be. As a result, they soar above the rest. Sometimes our life can be like an eagle's. There will be countless difficulties that we must choose to soar through and be able to embrace each and every season. But soaring is never easy. It takes hard work and determination!

What I've been learning in my own life is this: if we want to dream again, first we need to learn to accept soaring. In other words, we must let go and let God. Surrendering our days and life to Him isn't easy. We must let go of our own wants and desires and completely surrender ourselves to His ultimate plan. It sounds easy, but living it out is a whole different thing.

One way to surrender to God is by declaring His promises and truths over our lives. Declare means to voice and proclaim. What we declare over ourselves will either move us forward or keep us stuck. We can start by declaring life-giving words like, "We are capable, we are chosen by God, we are loved, and we are daughters of the King!" Another way to surrender is by being open to let God lead our everyday life. As I studied the life of an eagle, I learned that an eagle will never surrender itself to its prey or what it is up against. Sometimes we tend to submit to the wrong things in our lives. Instead of surrendering to God, we submit to our feelings, frustrations and fears and allow those things to lead our life, instead of God. But if we are going to move forward with the dreams in our hearts, surrendering our days to Him is going to be crucial. I love that Isaiah 40:31 tells us, "But those who wait upon God get fresh strength. They spread their wings and soar like eagles, they run and don't get tired, they walk and don't lag behind." The Lord will help us soar over the hardships that come at us. Surrendering to God will give us fresh strength and allow us to keep pushing through our daily life!

Another lesson I learned as I studied the life of an eagle is that eagles pick up on the everyday life challenges they encounter. And this affects how eagles respond to soaring. As we soar through surrendering, we must know that our character will be challenged. How we choose to respond to the challenge matters. We can't forget that our character is the cause for our construction. This key point is probably my favorite, but also the hardest to obey God on. As we grow in our character, God is at work constructing His plans for our lives. The definition of construction is the building of something typically large. As we surrender our spirit, mind, and body, He can move on with the construction of our life. Construction can be tedious and hard work, but it's in the construction that God moves in our lives and brings the big and little pieces together. When we stay faithful and obedient, He forms our life the way He planned it!

As we learn to surrender, we must let go and allow God to guide us through our life and let Him take the lead in our construction. He will help us renew our strength and allow us to soar like never before! So, let's not delay. Now is our time to soar.

Reflection

1. What is one area of your life that you can SURRENDER over to God today?

2. What is one way you can make your relationship with the Lord new and fresh?

Application

1. Get 1-2 women next to you that will inspire you as you grow in character and move closer to the dreams God has placed in your heart. Encourage and empower each other in surrendering your whole lives to God.

Adelynn Lammers

Day 18
Walking the Tightrope

Now faith is being sure of what we hope for and certain of what we do not see. This is what the ancients were commended for.
Hebrews 11:1-2 NIV

Have you ever watched someone walk across a tightrope over a high and dangerous spot with no net to catch them? I watched this happen one time on live television and I have never felt so much anxiety in my life. And I wasn't even the one walking the rope. Sometimes I think that's what pursuing a dream God has placed in our hearts feels like. Like we are walking the tightrope over a high and dangerous spot with no net to catch us. There was once a great tightrope walker named Blondin. He was one of the greatest tightrope walkers of all time, and there are many legends told of the feats he performed.

One of the most often told stories of Blondin concerns his crossing over Niagara Falls on a tightrope. He reportedly did that several times. At some point he turned to his large audience, which included numerous reporters from various newspapers, and he asked them, "How many have faith that I can walk across this tightrope over the Falls pushing a wheelbarrow?" People cheered loudly as they were sure the great Blondin could do it. Then he asked, "How many have faith that I can push a wheelbarrow across the tightrope with a man sitting in it?" Again, there was a loud response. Blondin then pointed to one of the most enthusiastic men in the audience, and said, "Okay, you get into the wheelbarrow." Needless to say, the man made a quick exit. His faith in Blondin was high until he thought he was going to be the man in the wheelbarrow.

I think we often do the same thing with God. We are enthusiastic in our faith that God can do impossible things. We are even enthusiastic that God can use someone else's life to do impossible things. But when God asks us to be the one to sit in the wheelbarrow and cross Niagara Falls, suddenly our faith can fail us. Blondin demonstrated that there is often a great difference between belief, the faith we SAY we have, and the action faith we really have.

This is what the ancients of the Bible were commended for. The kind of faith that had action. The kind of faith that took risks. The kind of faith that didn't just cheer each other's dreams on, but also stepped out into their own. The Bible says about Noah in Hebrews 11:7 *"By faith Noah, when warned about things not yet seen, in holy fear built an ark to save his family."* Noah didn't just believe God about the coming flood, but he actually began to obey God's command to build an ark. Sometimes we are waiting on a guarantee from God instead of just asking him for a command.

When it comes to stepping out in faith and taking some steps for God I think we fail to remember one very important thing. Yes we may be on a tightrope in a wheelbarrow above the Niagara Falls, but we can't forget, it's God that's pushing the wheelbarrow. God has never failed and He has never fallen. When God puts a dream in your heart, you can trust Him. When God asks you to take a step in faith, you can trust Him. When God asks you to take some risks, you can trust Him. And when God points at the wheelbarrow and tells you to get in, you can trust Him. He's going to get you across to the other side. And what an amazing trip it will be. Don't just stand on the sidelines and enthusiastically cheer for everyone else. Jump in the wheelbarrow and let God push you across. He will get you there.

Reflection

1. What is a crazy idea God has put in your heart?

2. What's the first step you may need to take?

Application

1. Today I encourage you to take a journal and start a bucket list if you don't have one. Prayerfully write down some crazy "tightrope walking" ideas you have or would like to accomplish. Begin to pray over those things and watch God open doors for them to happen. If you already have a bucket list add one more idea to it today.

Justeina Brownlee

Day 19
Embracing the Small Beginnings

*Do not despise these small beginnings, for the Lord rejoices to see the work begin. **Zechariah 4:10***

What are you dreaming about? Maybe you can recall dreaming big as a child. But now that you're older have you put your dreams on the back burner? Or even decided to abandon them altogether? Do you have one excuse after another for why you're not pursuing your purpose? Have you convinced yourself you don't have enough time, money, resources, skills, abilities, courage, faith and so on?

I love this reminder from Zechariah 4:10- *Do not despise these small beginnings, for the Lord rejoices to see the work begin.* "Despise" means to regard as worthless. But "rejoice," on the other hand, means to feel great joy and delight in. Small beginnings that you and I tend to consider as having very little value actually cause the Lord to rejoice. God specializes in using weak instruments to bring about mighty things. We can lose sight of the importance of small beginnings in every aspect of our lives. But great things come from a willingness to take small steps. God can take what little we have and do something great with it. Whatever we can offer of our time, abilities, and resources, the Lord can multiply its effectiveness beyond our wildest expectations.

The Lord has placed so much purpose within each of us. But how are we stewarding it? And what happens when our dreams don't unfold in a way that looks as amazing or as magnificent as someone else we know? We have to be so careful not to be distracted by comparison. The manner in which we live out the dreams God's given us is going to look different from others. But guess what? God designed it that way. So instead of allowing comparison to defeat us, we can give thanks and celebrate this fact.

Keep dreaming. We are never too old and it's never too late. And if not you, then who? If not now, then when? Take a step. Don't focus on the size of the step. Just step forward. Even when you don't feel like you're ready- take a step. We live in a "go big or go home" world, don't we? But God wants to prosper us in the little things. What we consider insignificant, God wants to use for a greater purpose.

I saw this quote recently, "The start is often what stops people." Did you catch that? It's the start that can trip us up. Small beginnings can disappoint us. Why? Because they often require hard work and little help. They're not all that glamorous. We can almost guarantee that we'll experience high resistance and opposition, and very little encouragement or fanfare. Small beginnings typically mean limited budgets and setbacks. We're not exactly lining up for small beginnings. But we can't forget that God's hand is all over the small beginnings.

It's okay if you haven't made the progress you thought you'd make by now. Remember that growth happens over time and typically not at warp speeds, but at more of a snail's pace. Let's agree to simply embrace the small beginning. To just begin right where we are and do what we can. And leave the results to God. He's got us!

Reflection

1. What excuses are keeping you in a place where you are despising the small beginnings? Who are you comparing yourself to when it comes to pursuing the dreams God's given you? How is this impacting or even paralyzing your ability to take the next step?

2. What small steps can you begin to take this week to step toward the dream(s) God's given you?

Application

1. Today, take a few minutes to write down some of the dreams God's laid on your heart. Pray and ask God to show you ways to embrace, rather than despise the small beginnings. Write down anything you sense God telling you. Consider sharing your reflection with a trusted friend or family member.

Leslie Meyer

Day 20
Let's get ready to Rumble

"Stay awake, stand firm in your faith, be brave, be strong."
1 Corinthians 16:13 CEB

When I hear this verse, I instantly relate it to a boxer in a boxing ring. In life, just like a boxing match, you'll have many punches thrown at you. But what you may not know is that in order to win the fight you must have a firm stance, a strategic mind, and corner men. These three things are essential at winning the fight.

So how does this relate to what I'm going through in life you might ask? If you're anything like me, you might have a dream or a task at hand that seems impossible. In the beginning, you approached it with such a passion and a fire. Then as the time goes on, that passion and fire you once had starts to dwindle. You forget the promises that God gave you. Your plan starts to get picked apart and thrown to the side of the road. The voices of others and your fears start to sway you in a different direction. You feel utterly defeated! But that is not God's intention for us in life! He created us to be victorious in our fight and this is how we win the fight.

Round 1: First things first, are you in fighting stance? When your doubts and fears start to kick in, when you're questioning if you've even heard God's voice, what are you telling yourself? What promises are you standing on? Jesus tells us this in John 16:33 "I have told you all this so that you may have peace in me. Here on earth you will have many trials and sorrows. But take heart, because I have overcome the world." Just like a boxer going into a fight, if your stance is not correct, if you are not rooted and planted in God's word you will fall. Once you get yourself rooted in God's word, the victory is yours.

Round 2: Who's in your corner? Are they life giving? Do they love the Lord and are they actively seeking Him in their lives? Are they telling you the hard truth or what you want to hear? Your corner men, your friends, who you're rollin' with, are essential to winning the battle. In a boxing match, your corner men are there to patch you up when you've gotten hurt. They see things in the fight that you can't see. They'll tell you if you're dropping your hands. Proverbs 15:22 says this "Refuse good advice and watch your plans fail; take good counsel and watch them succeed." So again I ask, who's in your corner?

Round 3: What's your battle plan? Every great boxer has an extremely strategic mind. They go into a fight with a plan at hand. They've learned their opponent's strengths and weaknesses. Just like a boxer, we can prepare ourselves for the fight at hand by being in God's presence. When we get quiet and we study His word, He lays out a plan before us. James 4:7 says "So humble yourselves before God. Resist the devil, and he will flee from you." When we're in God's presence all doubts, all fears, all those voices, they leave!

What we learned from being in the fight is this: we need a firm foundation in God's word. We need people in our corner that are not only going to encourage us, but will tell us what we need to hear not what we want to hear. We learn to get in God's presence so that He can lay out a plan before us! We learn that the victory is ours, that our dream is not impossible. We learned that in order to dream again we have to fight.

Reflection

1. Do you have a promise to stand on?

2. Do you have the right people in your corner? Are they pushing you forward?

3. Have you allowed God to give you a battle plan?

Application

1. Spend some time in God's presence and word. Allow Him to show you the promises that He has for you, direct you to the right corner men, and a write up a battle plan for your victory.

Marti Garrett

Day 21
Trailblazing

On the third day, officers went through the camp giving these instructions: "When you see the priests carrying the Ark of God, follow them. You have never before been where we are going now, so they will guide you. However, stay about a half mile behind, with a clear space between you and the Ark; be sure that you don't get any closer."
Joshua 3:2-4 TLB

You have never been where you are going now. That's the purest definition of trailblazing. To go places you've never been, try things you've never tried, dream things you've never dreamed. To do that takes one secret ingredient: Courage. Over and over in scripture, God commanded (not suggested) Joshua to be strong and courageous. That's because Joshua was a trailblazer. And trailblazing takes courage. God knew that he was sending Joshua and the Israelites places they had never been and they would need courage to get there. He was sending them from the wilderness they had known for the past forty years into the Promised Land in which they had never set their foot. He was sending them from a place where he provided all the food they needed through manna and never let their clothes wear out, into a place that they would have to plant their own crops, care for their own land and provide their own food. The same is true when God places a big dream in our hearts. It's usually a place we've never been and an idea we've never tackled. It's a place where we may have to work more, not less. It's a place that is going to take courage to get there. It's a place that we will have to blaze a trail.

What I love about God is that He didn't send Joshua out trailblazing without a promise to get him there. Scripture says in, Joshua 1:1-6 *"After Moses the Lord's servant died, the Lord spoke to Joshua, Nun's son. He had been Moses' helper. ² "My servant Moses is dead. Now get ready to cross over the Jordan with this entire people to the land that I am going to give to the Israelites. ³ I am giving you every place where you set foot, exactly as I promised Moses. ⁴ Your territory will stretch from the desert and the Lebanon as far as the great Euphrates River, including all Hittite land, up to the Mediterranean Sea on the west. ⁵ No one will be able to stand up against you during your lifetime. I will be with you in the same way I was with Moses. I won't desert you or leave you. ⁶ Be brave and strong, because you are the one who will help this people take possession of the land, which I pledged to give to their ancestors."*

Joshua wasn't trailblazing into a new Promised Land empty handed- God had equipped him with a very detailed promise. God promised that He would be with Joshua, that He wouldn't leave him, that He would give him every place he stepped, and that no one would be able to stand against them. So yes, Joshua was going places he had never been before, but he wasn't going without a promise from the One who would help him get there. When it comes to dreaming, it's much like trailblazing. We are going into territory we have never been. But we aren't going without a promise from the One that can get us there. If God has placed a dream in your heart and told you to go take possession of it, you can trust Him. He will be with you, He won't leave you, He will give you every step you take, and no one will be able to stand against that dream. There's just one secret ingredient you'll need. Courage. Joshua 1:9, *"Have I not commanded you? Be strong and courageous. Do not be afraid; do not be discouraged, for the Lord your God will be with you wherever you go."*

Reflection

1. What about trailblazing seems the scariest?

2. How would you rate your courage level as it relates to trying new things?

Application

1. Today spend some time in prayer asking God to give you a specific verse and promise from the Bible that aligns with the dream He has placed in your heart. Write that verse down and begin to memorize it so you can have it ready when you face uncertain times moving toward your promise land.

Justeina Brownlee

Day 22
Let Me Be Usable

*I BESEECH you therefore, brethren, by the mercies of God, that ye present your bodies a living sacrifice, holy, acceptable unto God, which is your reasonable service. **Romans 12:1***

What is God's will for your life? God has called each one of us to be a living sacrifice. A living sacrifice is living and not a dead sacrifice. God implores us to commit our lives to Him so He can display and prove His will for us. In Romans 12, Paul tells us that we have to "present" ourselves, that we have to choose, and commit our lives to God in order for His perfect will to manifest. This is not a vocation or specific service we should be considering, but a complete surrender to our Lord. On a daily basis we have to die to self and our sinful desires. This level of sacrifice or commitment is for each one of us to obtain. Jesus died for us, so we should live for Him. Once we make a decision to commit our lives to Christ, a process immediately begins in which we grow in our beliefs, desires and faith. This is a process that shows us who He is and who He says we are as we draw closer and talk with Him more. God prepares us to be usable which will lead into a vocation or special service for our Father and His Kingdom. God wants to use us greater than we can ever want or imagine. BUT remember that God wants US, our hearts, not just our service.

And be not conformed to this world: but be ye transformed by the renewing of your mind, that ye may prove what is that good, and acceptable, and perfect, will of God. Romans 12:2

So how do we demonstrate our commitment to the Lord? Well we can't be conformed to the pattern of this world. We need to separate ourselves to avoid destruction and live the life God has planned for us. If we like the world and follow that example, we will get the same results as them. 2 Peter 1:4 says we have been given exceedingly great and precious promises so that we can be partakers of the divine nature and escape the corruption of lust that belongs to the world. God wants a transformation to take place in our lives by the renewing of our minds. In the same way that we look in a mirror to see if our makeup is on right, the Word of God is a mirror to show us who we are in Christ. In I Thessalonians 5:23 it tells us God wants to sanctify us completely. When we are born again our spirit is made new and the process of sanctification for our soul begins; this will have a return that edifies the body. In order for this process to be effective it requires a constant renewing of the mind and fellowship with Him which will allow peace to come and plant itself in our soul. God wants us to be all in. In Isaiah 55:8-9 God tells us that our thoughts are not like His and that His ways are higher than our ways. After salvation this is when we choose to be a living sacrifice and separate ourselves from the world; proving that which is the good, acceptable and the perfect will of God. As we become more like him we become usable for the kingdom with desires that He gives us and dreams for our future.

Reflection

1. Are you following Jesus or are you expecting Jesus to follow you?

2. Are you separated from the world, are you feeding and renewing your mind with the Word?

Application

1. Daily spend 7 minutes in the morning to read scripture before you start your day. Seven minutes in the Word can change your life. Begin a new habit and receive all He has for you. You'll crave more. This will give you a new way of thinking, new desires and reveal His will for your life. Dreams will come true.

2. Separate yourself from this world and possess those things that are eternal. God wants you to be a living sacrifice and be totally sold out for Him.

Janet Conley

Day 23
Hearts Enlightened... Again

"Having the eyes of your hearts enlightened, that you may know what is the hope to which he has called you, what are the riches of his glorious inheritance in the saints, and what is the immeasurable greatness of his power toward us who believe, according to the working of his great might." **Ephesians 1:18-19**

The Apostle Paul knew of the lies the enemy would use to infiltrate our minds. So, he specifically prayed for the church in Ephesus that the "eyes of their heart would be enlightened" and "that they might know the beautiful things that God has for them". When I read that, the word imagination comes to mind. I believe part of the New Covenant involves dreams and visions, because I believe God wants His children dreaming and believing again for the "immeasurable greatness of his power".

So many times I will feel my imagination being enlightened, but I will allow fear, disappointments or loss of acceptance from others to cause me to stop opening my heart (or imagination) to the dreams I believe God has given me. I recently read this quote by Dale Turner, his words spoke deeply to me: "Dreams are renewable, no matter what our age or condition, there are still untapped possibilities within us and new beauty waiting to be born". It is one thing to dream, yet another to see the dream come true. Many times, I have shared my dream and it has fallen on "unsafe ears" or I shared the dream, before the whole detail of the dream was given. I was let down (or even hurt) because the response I was looking for from the "unsafe ears" was not given to me. Quite possibly, I shared the dream prematurely, leading to my own pain and frustration. I believe sometimes the dreams God gives us are meant to be private- just between you and Him. This has happened to me, which caused me to stop dreaming or allowing my imagination to experience "the immeasurable greatness of his power toward us who believe".

Many times it was past mistakes and failures that have caused me not to have an active imagination in my heart. I find these were some of my loneliest days. The past year, I have become a dreamer again. I have refocused and rearranged my life to hear from God and follow the dreams He has placed in my heart and mind, no matter if anyone else believed or understood the dream. This year, I have learned to hear God through the dream. I have learned how important it is to be still and quiet and to shut out the noise, so that I can hear Him clearly.

I took a missions trip to Belize that changed my life forever. It started as a dream and ended in reality. My husband and I have sold most of our belongings to start on a new journey of what we are calling our "Next". What started as a dream has become a reality. And while we do not yet have all the answers, we are learning to keep dreaming, keep trusting and keep believing in His Word.

I challenge you to no longer give the enemy space in your heart and mind to dampen your God-given dreams and imagination. We have the power to not just dream, but we have the power of the Holy Spirit to see our dreams come true, "according to the power of his great might".

Reflection

1. What are some of the ways you allow the enemy (or "unsafe ears") to stop you from obtaining your dream?

2. What are some of the dreams that scare you, because they look too big?

Application

1. Ask God daily to help you dream again. Ask Him to protect your heart, your mind, and the dream He gave you.

2. Spend quiet time daily allowing your heart to imagine and feel the dream God has given you. Pray for clarity, wisdom and open doors. Even if it looks impossible. Reflect on Ephesians 1:18-19.

Crystal Barnett

Day 24
Spying out Your Dream

Then Caleb silenced the people before Moses and said, "We should go up and take possession of the land, for we can certainly do it". But the men who had gone up with him said, "We can't attack those people; they are stronger than we are." And they spread among the Israelites a bad report about the land they had explored. **Numbers 13:30-32**

They had just been rescued out of 400 years of slavery. They had walked through the Red Sea and had watched the Egyptian army drown. They had been miraculously guided through the wilderness and been promised a land flowing with milk and honey. Eleven days after God gave them His Law and His promises, the children of Israel arrived at the border of the Promised Land. God told them clearly...go in and possess the Land. In other words, go in and get the Dream.

As they stood on the border of their dream, Moses and Aaron chose 12 men, the top leaders out of hundreds of thousands, to explore the land and see if God was telling the truth. The Bible adds an interesting statement and tells us that it was someone else's idea to go and spy out the land. Not really God's. After 40 days they returned with evidence: "We went into the land to which you sent us, and it does flow with milk and honey! Here is its fruit. (Numbers 13:27). Except then the scripture tells us that they didn't stop there, but instead went on to give all the reasons they would never be able to possess the dream. Every reason was based on fear. Based on insecurity. Based on a willingness to settle where they were. Based on their flesh. They all began to spread a bad report. Well...all but 2 of them.

There's a heavy-duty lesson for us in how the 12 spies reacted to the Promised Land. Remember, these 12 men traveled throughout the same land. They saw the same things. They were called to follow the same Dream. But they came to two very different conclusions. Joshua and Caleb saw scary things and trusted God, encouraging the Israelites to believe God's promises: "Let us go up at once and take possession, for we are well able to overcome" (v. 30). The other 10 spies saw scary things and doubted God (v. 31-33): "We are not able to go up against the people, for they are stronger than we." They said they saw giants "and we were like grasshoppers in our own sight ..."

How can two sides experience all the same things and have two different conclusions? How can two people be following the same dream with the same resources and the same gifts yet have two different outcomes? It all points back to what they decided as they stood on the border of their dream. When God places a dream or an idea or promise in our hearts, he actually doesn't want us to go spy out the land. He simply tells us to trust Him and go in and take possession of it. To move towards it. To take steps of faith. But instead we often, just like the 12 spies, decide to go explore and examine if we think the dream is really a possibility. Of course, the dream isn't possible. At least not on your own. But God doesn't leave us on our own to take possession of the dream. He already knows how He's going to make it happen. Today don't stand on the border of the land God has placed on your heart and try to explore it. Don't ask yourself if it's possible. Don't begin to allow the idea to form in your heart that the dream is too giant to possess. Just trust God and begin to take steps towards it. Commit in your heart just as Caleb and Joshua did... "We should go up and take possession of the land, for we can certainly do it." (Vs 30). God will take care of the rest. If you fast forward 40 years later, the only two spies that made it to the Dream were Joshua and Caleb. All because they didn't allow themselves to stand on a bad report. They trusted God.

Reflection

1. Who we surround ourselves with as we look at our dream makes a big difference. Only 2 of the spies could see beyond the giants and what God could do. Who do you have with you on your journey to seeing your dream come to life?

2. What giants do you see standing in the way as you look at your dream?

Application

1. As you look at the list of giants that seem to be standing in the way of your dream, attach what God would say about each of those giants. For example, if a giant in the way of your dream is that you don't feel qualified to do what God has called you to do, God would say "My grace is sufficient for you, for my power is made perfect in weakness". 2 Corinthians 12:9.

Justeina Brownlee

Day 25
Wisdom, Revelation & Enlightened Hearts

I keep asking that the God of our Lord Jesus Christ, the glorious Father,
may give you the Spirit of wisdom and revelation, so that you may
know Him better. I pray that the eyes of your heart may be enlightened
in order that you may know the hope to which He has called you...
Ephesians 1:17-18 NIV

In his letter to the Ephesians, Paul tells them of a beautiful and powerful prayer he prays for them. Why not pray a similar prayer for ourselves and for others when it comes to the dreams God has placed in our hearts?

We first see that Paul keeps "asking that the God of our Lord Jesus Christ, the glorious Father, may give you the Spirit of wisdom and revelation, so that you may know Him better". (Ephesians 1:17). Wisdom and Revelation... Who wouldn't want that prayed over them? Wherever you are in your dream process, it's so crucial to gain wisdom and revelation. We need wisdom to move in our dream the way God calls us. When we have wisdom, we know when to move and when to stay still. With wisdom we have the ability to discern whether an opportunity is God advancing us in our dream, or the enemy providing a distraction to deter us from reaching our dream. We need revelation to fully receive the dream and all that God has for us. When God gives us revelations about our dreams, we get to more fully see the big picture of the dream. Most importantly, we see in this passage of scripture that Paul isn't even focused on circumstances (or dreams). He knows we need the Spirit of wisdom and revelation *so we know God better*! God is more important than any dream He gives us.

We also read that Paul prays for hearts to be enlightened. "I pray that the eyes of your heart may be enlightened in order that you may know the hope to which He has called you, the riches of His glorious inheritance in His holy people, and His incomparably great power for us who believe" (Ephesians 1:18-19). Paul prays that the Ephesians will have the eyes of their hearts enlightened. Enlightened means to be given greater knowledge and understanding about a subject or situation, to be given spiritual knowledge or insight. The Amplified Bible provides such a good visual, it says, "having the eyes of your heart flooded with light." Think of being in a dark room. You don't know what else is in there. You can assume there is furniture, but unless you've been in that room before you don't know what kind of furniture, or what color of furniture, or the room could even be a completely empty room. Suddenly, you notice a light is turned on somewhere outside the room so now there's a little bit of light coming in under the door and you can definitely tell there is furniture in the room, but you can't determine anything else. Until suddenly the door swings open, the light is turned on, and your eyes are flooded with light so you can clearly see everything. You no longer have to guess or assume anything, you now fully know.

This is Paul's prayer, that the eyes of their heart would be flooded with light. That they wouldn't have to assume there's a hope or think there might be a hope to which they've been called, but that their hearts would be so softened that the light would come flooding in and they would know without a doubt the hope and the future God has for them and the power they have in God. This should be our continual prayer.

Reflection

1. How would your life and dreams change if you began praying a prayer like Paul's?

2. How can you redirect your thinking and prayers to be more focused on God and the power He's given you?

Application

1. In your prayer time today begin praying that God would give you the Spirit of wisdom and revelation, and that the eyes of your heart would be enlightened. Continue to pray this over yourself and others daily.

Erin Killion

Day 26
Dream Big

*"For I know the plans I have for you," declares the Lord, "plans to prosper you and not to harm you, plans to give you a hope and a future." **Jeremiah 29:11***

Do you ever sit down under a warm blanket with a cup of coffee or hot chocolate and ask yourself, what's next? What's my dream? What dream did God put in my heart? I used to, but if I am going to be completely honest with you, I hadn't done that for a long time until a friend recently asked me what my dream was? Now, let me tell you, this sweet girl looked me dead in the eye wanting an answer, like now, and she wanted a good answer. She didn't want any old general answer that I was really good at giving! You know the ones, "I want my children to love and serve the Lord and I want a happy, fun loving marriage that honors God first and a healthy family and I want to serve God and please him every day of my life!" You know those answers too, don't you? Don't get me wrong, I want all of those things. But oh no, she wanted to know what my dream was, one that I could not accomplish on my own, a BIG dream, a God sized dream. There was no easing into it. No small talk. Just jumping right in early one Tuesday morning. She asked again, "So, what's your Dream? I think you stopped dreaming and God is saying He wants you to dream again!" I was speechless and had no answer (and if you know anything about me, this is a rare occurrence!) My mind started to wander, and my wheels really started to turn. 'What IS my dream? Wow God, she is right. You are right!' Girls, it is time to dream again and I want YOU to join me!

I don't know about you, but when I was a little girl, my heart was filled with dreams. BIG dreams, God sized dreams. I wanted nothing more than to grow up and be on the stage at Disney World, singing and dancing as Belle for all the children in the Magic Kingdom. The following year, I wanted to be a Radio City Rockette and the year after that, I wanted to be an Olympic Ice Skater. At that time, the sun was the limit as to what I could do and what I could be. Dreaming came easy to me! Why was it so different now? What had changed in me? What has changed in you?

So, my question to you is, are you still dreaming? Are you dreaming those God sized dreams or have you been where I was and allowed life to swallow some of those childlike dreams for your future? If your answer to these questions is like mine, then you're in luck, because today all of that changes for you. There is so much more to life than you are living and that begins with big dreams. Today God is using this devotion, to knock on your door and tell you it's time to dream again! You may be asking, but how? Start by spending time with God and asking Him to help you dream again. Spend time in His word, worshipping, and listening to that still small voice of the Holy Spirit inside of you. God has placed a desire in your heart to do what only you can do! These dreams are an essential part of who He created you to be!

In John 15:5, Jesus said "I am the vine; you are the branches. If you remain in me and I in you, you will bear much fruit; apart from me you can do nothing." Apart from Him you can do nothing, which means with him you can accomplish anything he calls you to. Do you want that childlike, God filled faith again? The kind that reminds you that you can do anything? I sure hope you are encouraged today and as excited as I am for you, because God has big plans ahead for you through these big dreams! Jeremiah 29:11 says, "For I know the plans I have for you," declares the Lord, "plans to prosper you and not to harm you, plans to give you a hope and a future." Rest in that today. Stand on His promise of hope for your big future. Big Dreams truly do await you!

Reflection

1. Have I stopped dreaming GOD sized dreams? If so, Why? What is getting in the way? Fear? Disbelief? Busyness? Settling for just ordinary life when it could be an extraordinary life?

2. What is God speaking to me today about my dreams? What is stirring in my heart right now?

Application

1. Ask God to expose what is keeping you from dreaming God sized dreams and to help you dream again with desires that align with His plan for your life.

2. Spend the next few weeks journaling what God is revealing to you. What desires are starting to stir in your heart? Start a list of these dreams and continually add to it. Then mark them off as God begins to move on your behalf. Your faith will be strengthened through this process.

Kelly Hopson

Day 27
Dreams Come True

One of them, when he saw he was healed, came back, praising God in a loud voice. He threw himself at Jesus' feet and thanked him—and he was a Samaritan. **Luke 17:15-16**

We should all dream. We should have goals and aspirations. I even have a list of dreams on my phone that I would love to accomplish someday. But do you realize when a dream you once had becomes a reality? When one of the dreams on my bucket list gets checked off, do I notice? Is the life you are living right now a dream that has come to life? I would admit that at times I have gotten so caught up thinking about my next dream that I have missed the opportunity to thank God for the dream I am living right now.

With each dream comes a new level of responsibility, a new level of work. If I am not careful, I can miss the dreams God has allowed me to live because of the work it takes to live that dream. For example, my kids are dreams that I once had. I remember being newly married and praying for God to bless me with a sweet baby girl, but she is work! At times, I can get caught up in parenting and miss the blessing that she is. I also dreamed that one day I would be able to leave my job and be a stay at home mom. I was blessed with that opportunity, but do I realize it or do I see the challenge of being home with my kids day in and day out? Am I missing the dream that has become a reality?

I think this can happen to all of us. Let's take a look an example found in Luke 17:12-19. "As Jesus was going into a village, ten men who had leprosy met Him. They stood at a distance and called out in a loud voice, "Jesus, Master, have pity on us!" When He saw them, He said, "Go, show yourselves to the priests." And as they went, they were cleansed." Let's pause there - I have to believe that all 10 of these men had dreamed they would be healed. I believe they had spent time imagining what it would be like to be healed. But what happens next in the story is what was interesting to me. "One of them, when he saw he was healed, came back, praising God in a loud voice. He threw himself at Jesus' feet and thanked him—and he was a Samaritan. Jesus asked, "Were not all ten cleansed? Where are the other nine? Has no one returned to give praise to God except this foreigner?" Then He said to him, "Rise and go; your faith has made you well." Did you catch that? Ten came to Jesus asking for the healing, the dream, but only ONE came back to thank Jesus for making the dream come true.

As I reflect on all that God has done for me, I can't help but to see how faithful He has been in my life. It reminds me that God is faithful, all the time! It reminds me that I want to be the one that runs back to my God and throw myself at His feet and thank Him.

Reflection

1. Think about some of the dreams you have prayed about. What dreams have come to life?

2. Are there any dreams that you once prayer for that have now come true? Do you need to run back to God and thank Him for those dreams?

Application

1. Get a journal and make a list of your dreams. Start to journal about your dreams and how God begins to answers your prayers and fulfill the dreams you have!

Betsy Baringer

Day 28
Do Not Be Afraid

*For God has not given us a spirit of fear and timidity, but of power,
love, and self-discipline.* ***2 Timothy 1:7 NLT***

When we share something repeatedly, we are trying to drive
home the importance of what we are saying. And when someone tells
us something more than once, we begin to sense that it must be quite
significant. Did you know that the command "do not fear" is written in
the Bible 365 times? Wow! God didn't want you and I to mess this one
up. He knew we would struggle with fear, worry, and anxiety over
situations and outcomes that we cannot control. He gave us as many
reminders as there are days in a year to speak life into the situations
we're facing that have us feeling most afraid. When we are afraid, we
experience fear and that fear fills us with apprehension. Fear starves
faith, but faith, on the other hand, starves fear. We get to choose
whether or not we are going to focus on our fears or our faith in God.
It's critical that we never lose sight of the fact that the size of our God
is always greater than the size of the problems we face.

You see, God wants us to know that He is with us. Fear sets in
when we depend on ourselves, our own performance, our own skills,
and our own strength instead of asking God to fill us with his courage
and supernatural power that enables us to face difficulty, danger,
pain, etc. despite our greatest fears. God has His eye on us. He's
looking for people like you and I to step out in faith, where it feels
uncomfortable, and even scary. He wants to show us that each and
every time we choose to trust Him, He gets a little bigger in our lives.
Not only will we gain insight on His magnificent power and ability to
bridge the gap, but we'll also experience His unfailing love, His
unexplainable peace, and His unending mercy, grace, and forgiveness.
He wants us to know that He is faithful. He can't wait for us to witness
more "But for God" moments in our lives. It doesn't mean that we'll
be spared from adversity, but we'll gain a new and deeper
understanding of who God is and all that He is capable of.

One of my favorite verses about fear is found in 2 Timothy 1:7
For God has not given us a spirit of fear and timidity, but of power,
love, and self-discipline. (New Living Translation). God wants to help

you and me overcome our fears so that we can do whatever it is He is calling us to do. Power, love, and self-discipline are available to each of us because the Holy Spirit lives inside us. Our faith grows most when we rely on God and trust in what we cannot see. It's uncomfortable, messy, and even inconvenient at times, but ALWAYS worth it! So today, let's declare our dependence on God, the creator, sustainer, deliverer, and redeemer of all things and thank Him for the power of His Holy Spirit to push past our fears. Together, let's commit to continuing to discover and live out our purpose.

Reflection

1. What or who are you putting your trust in? In what ways are you allowing fear to keep you from doing what you sense God is calling you to do? What are you clinging to and finding safety and security in apart from God?

2. What are you most in fear of leaving behind if you step out in faith and why? Is it your job? Approval from others? Having enough financial resources? Fear of failure?

Application

1. Find verses that speak to God's faithfulness and provision and write them down to refer back to when fear creeps in.

2. Journal about the specific gifts God has blessed you with. Consider how you can be more bold, loving, and self-disciplined with the gifts you've been given by God. Talk with a trusted friend about what God is revealing to you.

Leslie Meyer

Day 29
Overcoming the Pain

'Jesus said, "Father, forgive them, for they don't know what they are doing". And the soldiers gambled for his clothes by throwing dice.'
Luke 23:34

Have you been hurt by someone in your life? Have people given up hope on you because you were different, or you made a mistake again? Or maybe you're the one sitting in the back of the room, feeling invisible because people left you out again. Do you feel like you will never amount to anything because people have spoken these words over your life numerous times? Have you tried to overcome the pain someone has caused you but didn't have success?

God can help you overcome the pain and hurt you may be feeling, but first we have to ask Him for this help. We cannot do it without His hands on it. He is sitting there waiting for us to ask, 'God can you help me overcome this hurt that I'm experiencing? I feel like I can't let go of the pain that is filling my heart and affecting the decisions I'm making. I know you are the only One that can take this and use this for good.' Maybe you have already prayed this prayer many of times, but you don't feel God has answered you. Sometimes God is trying to speak to us through our pain and we are missing it.

When I think of the pain and hurt I have experienced by loved ones, I try to reflect on Jesus and everything he had to endure. Jesus was brutally beaten, far worse than anything I could ever imagine. The soldiers placed a crown of thorns on His head, piercing his skull. They whipped him with a leather strap, which was made of small pieces of bone and metal. They would soak the whip in water to make it even heavier. When they whipped him, the leather whip would pierce his flesh, ripping his skin, and exposing tissue and bone. As if that pain wasn't enough, Jesus then had to carry the cross to where he would be crucified. Once they arrived at skull hill, Jesus would then have to face nails being driven into his wrists and feet.

During all of this physical pain Jesus had to endure, they were mocking and saying hurtful things to him. Jesus endured far more pain and hurt than you and I will ever come across. Yet in the midst of all they had done to him, Jesus, as he is hanging from the cross with people mocking him and his body in excruciating pain, says 'Father, forgive them, for they do not know what they are doing'. WOW! I don't know about you, but if I had to go through what Jesus went through, I'm pretty sure I would not be able to say forgive them! But Jesus' heart is so pure and great! Maybe, just maybe, if we can look through the eyes and heart of Jesus, we can make it one step closer to overcoming our pain and hurt.

What does pain have to do with a dream? Without pushing past the pain and making it to the other side of forgiveness, your heart is not free to dream. Even if the dream is that one day you will be able to forgive someone who hurt you, be able to forgive yourself for hurting someone you love, or just healing from past events, you can take those steps towards that dream today!

Reflection

1. Who has hurt or caused you pain in your life? Have you been able to forgive them? If you haven't, what are some ways you can work toward forgiving them?

2. Pain is inevitable. It will happen, whether someone hurts you international or unintentional, hurt and pain will come. What steps can you put into place now that will help you forgive or overcoming the pain and hurt when it does come knocking?

Application

1. When someone hurts you, because you know this will happen in our lives, remember all the suffering Jesus had to go through for you. Remember that none of us are perfect and we all have hurt someone.

Brittani Lime

Day 30
Through People Like Me?

Jesus said, "You are tied down to the mundane; I am in touch with what is beyond your horizons. You live in terms of what you see and touch. I'm living on other terms." **John 8:23**

Do you ever feel ordinary? As women, we often feel like we work, we mom, and we wife. Daily we fight the fight of exhaustion, inadequacy, anxiety, fear, and worry. I personally feel like I'm never enough in one day. Most often, I am a failure, my parenting lacks, my patience is short, and my fuse is shorter. I've worked my whole life to hide the deep, dark, dirty, and shameful pieces of myself. I fear the day that someone sees who I think the real me is. If I am being honest, I often think how or why would God choose me when I am quite sure there are so many better candidates. Can you relate? Are you constantly bogged down with the shame and guilt of never being enough?

Lies! When God is looking for someone to use, we assume that we aren't what He is looking for. It is easy to give God all the reasons why we don't meet the qualifications on His biblical job description. It's easy to believe the lies that Satan uses to help us determine that we aren't worthy of being used. Lies like: we aren't qualified, we can't do this, we're not capable, we will fail, etc. Satan uses these lies to strip the power of God from us or to work through us because our insecurities take over. We don't even have the option of considering we might be enough, because we already know we aren't. When we listen to the lies that Satan uses to take away from our worth, we make ourselves unavailable to the blessings that God has in store for our lives.

When God is looking for the qualified, He isn't looking for the person who might have it all together, but rather the person who is willing to learn and grow into the person He wants us to be; because when we change, His power becomes evident. He's looking for the person who will acknowledge that they would fall short if it weren't for Him. Truthfully, if we felt like we accomplished something, we would accept the credit. When our skills are lacking, He takes over and makes us look put together. All we have to be is willing to use the talents God gives and nurtures within us. Are you willing? If God is asking you to step out, to do something, would you do it, despite what you think about yourself or what you believe yourself to be? His only job description is a willing heart, capable of identifying His truth in order for Him to move in our lives.

Do you recognize that Satan purposefully uses lies to separate us from the truth of God's word, to separate us from God's vision, and to divide us from the will of God? We are more susceptible to lies when there is no truth to guide us. It is imperative that we begin to look at the lies Satan uses to hold us down and replace those lies with truth! The truth is, in Christ, we were made in His image, we are not a mistake, we are altogether beautiful, we are powerful, we have a sound mind, we are more than conquerors, we are chosen, and we cannot be separated from His love.

Imagine the powerful force we would be if we believed what God said about us! Wash those lies off of you today and become a willing participant in the move of God in your life. Allow Him to tear down those insecurities, declaring one truth at a time and be open to His calling. Watch Him erase those fears, watch your weaknesses turn into His strengths and watch as He develops you into His version of enough!

Reflection

1. Do you believe that God thinks you are qualified?

Application

1. Take time to write some of the lies you believe about yourself and replace them with God's truth!

Heather Westrick

My Dream Bucket List

_____

_____

_____

_____

_____

_____

_____

_____

_____

_____

_____

_____

_____

_____

_____

_____

_____

_____

My Dream Bucket List

_____

_____

_____

_____

_____

_____

_____

_____

_____

_____

_____

_____

_____

_____

_____

_____

_____

My Dream Bucket List

_____

_____

_____

_____

_____

_____

_____

_____

_____

_____

_____

_____

_____

_____

_____

_____

_____

_____

My Dream Bucket List

_____

_____

_____

_____

_____

_____

_____

_____

_____

_____

_____

_____

_____

_____

_____

_____

_____